Lois
Pereiro

Collected Poems

LOIS PEREIRO

Collected Poems

Translated from Galician by Jonathan Dunne

XUNTA DE GALICIA　　　　　　　　Small Stations Press

Small Stations Press
Registered address: 20 Dimitar Manov Street, 1408 Sofia, Bulgaria
You can order books and contact the publisher at
www.smallstations.com

Poems © María Inés Pereiro Pontón, 2011
English translation © Jonathan Dunne, 2011
Cover photograph © Manuel Vilariño, 2011
Design © Yana Levieva, 2011
© Small Stations Press, 2011
© Xunta de Galicia, 2011

The three books included in this volume were first published in Galician as *Poemas para unha Loia* (Espiral Maior, Coruña 1997), *Poemas 1981/1991* (Edicións Positivas, Santiago de Compostela 1992) and *Poesía última de amor e enfermidade 1992-1995* (Edicións Positivas, Santiago de Compostela 1995).

The publishers wish to express their gratitude to the author's brother, Xosé Manuel Pereiro, for his invaluable help. The quotation from Gérard de Nerval's "El Desdichado" on page 118 is translated by Donald Swann

This English edition first published in 2011, reprinted in 2017
ISBN 978-954-384-007-6 (paperback original)
ISBN 978-954-384-069-4 (reprint edition)
All rights reserved. The content of this work is protected by the law, which prohibits the reproduction, plagiarism, distribution or public communication, in whole or in part, of a literary, artistic or scientific work, or its transformation, interpretation or artistic performance fixed in any kind of medium or communicated through any means, without the proper authorization

Contents

7_ Poems for a Skylark

37_ Poems 1981/1991

85_ Last Poetry of Love and Illness 1992-1995
  89_ 1. Posthumous Poems (1992-94)
  105_2. Light and Shadows of Love Revived (1995)
  163_3. Poems of Death Survived by Means of Passion and Sabotage (1995)

Poems for a Skylark*

---

* *Skylark* (*Loia* in Galician) was the name of a magazine edited by the author and others in Madrid between 1975 and 1978, which is where the following poems first appeared.

Conversation with Pablo

Out the back, beaten boxes
Here
two eyes watch the hatchet
leaning in the kitchen.

Then clearly seeing how it approaches
and kills
how it approaches and kills
                                  and kills
And Pablo those days
so much blood
so many shouts on your death
at the funerals. They were days
Pablo dead, of silence,
       (How it approaches and kills…)
of silence.

Alan's Psychedelic Breakfast

Yeah, do me a favour, a
hit in this ear. Who gifts
the unreality of being myopic?
Each hand
in its appearance

Exactly a house that burns

Traitors wounded me
in your footsteps in the street.
The exactness of the house that burns

Because
in the rhythm of bells, is it worth being reflected?
Psychedelic
Psychedelic
        (Repeat)
What's that?
It isn't worth it.
I know what's waiting for me when
I return.
Please, is it worth it?
Drink a bit

    lying on the grass
        loving each other in the captive
            cow's mouth…

That

That night
I took the hand by the cold of the fingers
and ran it gently over my lips
wanting to find the signs
of the last aborted cries
when even blood didn't remember
the joy of marble
under tickling fear

Why, love?

All was quiet…

Conspiracy against Lois

> *We cannot lengthen our existence.*
> *Death is unforgiving.*
>
> Vladimir Mayakovsky

And you
(nail that image to your eyes)
the
ethereal
solution
of suicide

Meeting with Piedad. Turn and Return of the Sun. I Love, You Love, He Loves

for Piedad, always

We needed to encourage the sun to appear. We needed to encourage the rain to appear. I thought by crying... But we had to sing as she did, like this:
—Wait for me
—Continue (the light is going, the light is going, the light is going)
—...
—Cross the mouth with your lips
(She turns around, turns a thousand times. Lands on death)
The same at all hours. I crossed her mouth with my lips. "There's no point complaining." I felt the force of her body penetrating the earth.
The Sun.
The sun has left us. The sun is free, the sun is not free. King Sun, Solthermic, *Oh waiting for the sun, waiting for the sun, waiting for the sun...*
Change
I love, you love, he loves M-o-t-h-e-r l-o-v-e-s m-e. Oedipus complex on the stairs.
I love, you love, he loves: Jim. I like gay looks.
I love, sweet Jim, you are if she taught me. The softness of sweet Jim's kisses at night. The sweetness of sweet Jim's kisses at night. Night, it's nine: I disappear
    Jim, will your corpse be sweet?
        I am stabbed
            Change

And you continue because in fact we all love each other. Imagine. When blood appears and we kill each other turning over the portrait remains. The exception proves the rule. Rule in fact we all hate each other. The exception is the rule.

    Imagine.
—"I love you"
—Kiss me
—Love me (the drops of water turn into blood!!! Not like that)
—...
(She turns around, turns a thousand times on my death)
The piano, when did pianos smell of death?
And she says, "why do pianos smell of death?"
The piano destroys me
    But in the end I cross her mouth with my lips. It's always the same, on and on until hate
    On and on until death: "I love you"
I know a person's desires
    Do you love me?
    Does Jim love me?

        And now all that
        is kisses
        on the lips
        Is kisses on the lips
        on the lips.

Children

The classic structure
of a crowd of captive women
their experiments with oppression
giving us a foot of dynamite
they should know the death of children
doesn't matter.

—R—

I recollect
the habit of dancing
when out of a bottle we will drink
or burn the wings of blue doves
when the white ones eternal pacifists
rise again
Paul Éluard.

Donald Barthelme Donald Barthelme

When you awake
death has arrived
when the sounds of waters
soon dead
the wings of glass
electrical hands
fall in love with the green eyes of mothers
thoughts
of a murderous son in love with his mother
for you to wake in silence etc.
Eric?

The Flowers of Friendship Faded Friendship Faded

We foresee the hours of summer
living by day
cold future dreams

of moon dawns and cold-eyed transparent wardrobes
murderers of sleeping princesses
in piles of innocent drinks
kings of solitary explosion
on a dark day for the country accused of wanting to be
dwarves and living on grass
aiming at you with death in decline
from the day of the journey
or sentimental flight
howling (the call of the wood which was hidden from me)
the sound
of desperate sense
tragic sound.

Ecstasy
in a smile seeing
how Piedad you killed that dark hole in the shape of a crime
where silence smells
of a nostalgic neurotic storm
                              (a neurotic centre but
one with a fixed border)
and it wasn't the first time
suicide had hung in the sky of the last landscape
Mary (*buked and scorned*)
had seen it before
in the sky of California.

After the Cold Weather

After the cold weather
you know we're lost
in a bit
of violence

the queens of the sleeping heart (a)
in the dark wood there's still fighting (b)
and outside the sea damp sand (c)

with which to feed the kids
I'd have with you
if a blue cloud came down to land

But after this
silence is left
at war

Dusk in Ireland

> *Lois, the potatoes don't taste like they used to,*
> *the harvest must be bad.*
> *Let it be again like the star*
> *when it talks.*
>
> Piedad

Of the magical solidity
of dancing chlorophyllic
cords
between the least long
the accurate tremor
and the call
of the greenest blackest
dearest dampest mountain
magical and solid
silk and decadent.

Rose Intransigent with Power

By night, body of curtains talking of opera
disturbs the old order
the new lover?
tall by night flown by day
everything is uncomfortable
between body and soul
that is hunchbacked Balbina between the sun hastening
      to arrive
and those in macs shooting
Four evocations of the moon.

Dyn Amo and Steve Dwoskin

feed me, my dear

Perfection of a game
In the confusion to know is to guess
Dyn Amo, false trail, neither murders nor is delirious
seduced and perfect in the game
of dressing in talc and gesture
Neither converts angels nor freezes the figure
neither shadow of a cloud nor mark of a diva
does a striptease:
marvellous lips fly over Europe
mistress of shows and virgins.

Possessed Lady

We are always in sinister lands
—begins the small guest—confusion
of plants tailor of dolls
It's not the king sticking his paws on the table
the greatest danger but that in the best days
of Tea
there should be more light the wrong Sun falls
paradise of slaves
shadow of glory.

Cobalt and Professor Calculus

Pale Rose
will be the new lover
if autumn comes and finds me weak
Calculus invents the bomb for no reason
and those in macs shooting
four evocations of the moon.

Butterflies Are Volvos

The light shrewd, Nico, shuddering of
abnormal triptych
complete and soaked
Without limit in tides
the passing Violet of boats without needle
or thread from beginning to end
from end to beginning
Prodigy of a minute?
while they see each other and sing a fear of
colour to loony bins
gaseous clothes when in the salary
of those who despise us
in the extension of the eye there exists
"that musical light perceived by the spirit"

feared and loved in innocence
they answer with atrocities,
four by four.

In Leonberg

> *Bid adieu, adieu, adieu,*
> *Bid adieu to girlish days.*
>
> James Joyce, *Chamber Music*

Bored
a smell of coffee
in the indifference of Prague.
Crested feathers, artificial green.
An exciting entry
for a final game of lovers.

A blue tenor sings the turn of the passion when
the only innocent falls.

Against an Egyptian backdrop
the head to one side, in profile.

Ein Menschheitsbuch

THOMAS MANN
TOMAC MAHH

What damp word in procession
allows a lover's vigil to be foreseen?
Heroic surrender of the body visited
by funeral figures from the feverish century
on the edge of a sick soul which rests.

Amorous refuge weaves the placid
face of merry victims,
of the duo possessed of a sense of honour,
Ah, a sense of honour!

Enter the current of Knowledge
with something tragic in its breast,
ghost of the shipwrecked future,
deep virtue on the road to perdition.

Lysistraphes. Altocumuli

> *Je t'adore à l'égal de la voûte nocturne,*
> *Ô vase de tristesse, ô grande taciturne.*
>
> Charles Baudelaire

From this grotto of sex and profane prayer
the slave of war's pacific shadow.
Authentic sky broken by love,
which only has to bleed to death.

> *As a lone ant from a broken ant-hill*
> *from the wreckage of Europe, ego scriptor.*
>
> Ezra Pound

1859 to 1861

Unravelling without glory the line of those faces
their imagined soul awakes
in the manner of slaves future lords.

The dark and misunderstood sign of beauty
enters from the body of my past page.

Thousands of seconds hanging
from the tangled climate
in the first cold season.
How often in the presence of a mirror
do you reject primordial objects?

That marked pleasure, gross, grey,
          weak, ephemeral…

Impression (*Lamentatio*) 1913-Spa

The first hand to be revealed,
grateful vision
were it not held up by the vengeful body,
opens the door of light of its home
and observes a sea of clouds
foreshadowing war.

The challenge trembles in two spirits,
for indignation grows
in the vision of healthy bodies
tired of being "sick humanity".

Parade on Bright Footsteps and Corpses

I
PRÉLUDE

A token of love could be
the tenebrous act of jabbing…

II
FEUX D'ARTIFICE

… but without its familiar stain.
Underneath the secrets everyone knows,
the fragile figure with the spirit of Atlas,
a clear head
follows the procession of life,
proof of war, delirium of commoners.
Mimsi Foer, that plucked molly cat,
Dalta Minoi, how much ignorance
in the chorus watching you.

Flee from us, air of madness,
perfect vision,
heap of vigil and clarity,
secret brand of known origin,
adoration and death
de profundis.

Gothic Thought

> Bach, *English Suite No. 3 in G minor*
> Satie, *Songe creux*

Cloistral sighs at the bottom of the moon
brought down in the inner cell's mirror.
The murmuring empire will reign
venerable sacrifice of howling saliva.

And the poisoned body walks the punishment
of blood grown by the strength of god.
Hidden in the nest of roses the ivy crown
turns to night in the appointed voice.

Ah! romantic character inclined to bodily strength
the countenance of misty epochs
wears your false expression
withered sign of human condemnation.

Helen Brigador, Terror of Saints

Enough treasure!
With happy footsteps and ill-fated calm
she makes converts of herself;
Helen Brigador
and hard-worked body,
her face protected by a veil,
an inclination of love in other habits.

Leonora in Confidence

Does she know what trees of mystery
adults twist with their preaching?
tongue moistened
on black brush,
illuminated darkens.

The day rests
in cold steel calm
better in you,
profaning maid
martyred mouth
prepared for greater loneliness.

Proposition

In time to tempt the main fall
I divest myself of glory and seed of wealth.
On the face of these primitive days,
in possession
of divine guilt
or mystery of Reason,
to write with delicacy
in a Pandora's box
of pain.

Poems 1981/1991

Atrocity Exhibition

Leave a kiss on the mirror
where my shadow burns at night
and let them rot together,
the image of your absence
silhouetted in red with your lips
and the violent profile of my dream
which engenders love grey smoke
crimson hatred
on tongue and teeth
blood and semen.

Two Minutes of Dancing Dervishes

> *Dir auch -: tauschen die Nächte*
> *dich in ein dunkleres Du...*
>
> Gottfried Benn

With the eternal dissidence
of omnipresent Arabic broadcasters
distilling small hour energy
you reconstruct the past in two minutes
—urgent and immoral like an internal
rhythmic obscenity transfusion—
intercepting engines of torture
in that ardent muscular atmosphere
infected with my depression
which grows old like a desert in Europe
in the presence of death on the epidermis
of a sinusoidal song
on Medium Wave.

Level

Halfway up cables in the vanguard
criss-crossing the air crossroads
anonymous perspectives without shade
level of smoke and fluids of the deformed
a suburb of steel and kilowatts
with the stature of procreated lands.

Corporal (*Je T'Aime...*)

The mouth's fury, teeth:
the arms of passion
which explore and profane the intact skin

Luxurious flesh
toxic
love injects

The cold congealed on hand and wound
tingles in rebellion
forms a scar
between the possible breasts
of another triumph

Every three seconds then
two eyelids lubricate
the hostile eyes that don't believe.

Cartography

As if dead already
or defeated
I talk beside myself
and sleep
in disaster

It should be possible
to make maps of hatred
and damp monologues
of night-time
cisterns
to decipher

Verschwende deine Jugend

It will be another invasion
to the inconstant mercury of the past
sharpened the knives of memory
in a savage present that instructs me

Raining only to wound
this definitive industrial night
of liquid needles in fierce unanimous attack
spitting its armoured acoustics
in this illegal insomnia
of etceteras.

Who?

Wim Wenders the same ritual
of gestures and sublime pauses
writing a retrospective manual
in the calm of European technology
fragments of epidemic committing me
to the flesh I know

I will be another day:
you come back,
to be me.

Quod nunc ratio est, impetus ante fuit.
Ovid, "Remedia Amoris"

Afterwards

Now penitence
shivers.
Everything closed sleeps and falsifies:
canned cold delayed fever.

Ether

The light fell out of the window
with the vast sea of morning feathers
to declare that all love is useless

while the icy curtain of your contempt
drips with savage rhythm.

Car Crash (of Negative Death)

In the shade of this metallic horror
you will write dialogues of the death
of memory's homicidal tickles
in the geometric centre of the crash
leaving the door open to other scenes
in the emulsion of my eyes exposing
images of accidents and wounds

Narcissism

I follow in the footsteps of my body's blood
and with my sturdiest fingernail
open a half-moon path
in the vein that bluely receives me

Penetration Prayer

Celebrate and receive
in the language of rage
on the limits of euphoria
in your mouth
this white gold and logical poison
with your blood half open
to an uncertain world
in fragmented doses of ruin

demolition
is the iron with which we are armed

celebrate nostalgia
and in the absence of vice
conserve your hate
condemn yourself
amen.

Dandy

The mirror of elegance before my eyes
and the eyelids sleep a sinewy sleep
in liquid lines of gestures drawn
on a face of cruelty close to mine

I turn into fear murderer
and as an angel passes *un ange passe*
everyone would like to see after the orgy
if what I've kept is a thought
threaded in needles of irony.

Lace of Inertia

The day my blood is strong enough
to wither and pluck the ivy of love
with firm footsteps
the inertia of habit will come
to weave me in disasters another style
with threads of emotion and sluggish needles
curing the new insanity
with the antidote of logic
leaving new nets on my sex
to keep the ivy alive
—its poison—
in the idea that destroys
the *ennui* that creates.

Nothing

With a gesture towards the body
the earth
and Nothing
they laid strange earth
on the accursed flower
of his worst image
on his corpse
in full possession of its future
with traces on its skin
of the silk-wrapped breath of a lover
present in her absence
frozen hands
a mortal perfume
and again nothing.

Six

From this wintry sky
more signs
for a regressive
metamorphosis

the fire flickers in sweet eyes
and there's a sixth shadow where there were five.

Remorse

The opium-smoking Monforte mist
is the mother of furtive silhouettes
and I greet the danger shining
on the dark face of your dreams
dropping the fatal tear in veins.

And sadly it doesn't sleep in the depth of eyes
prophecies growing in the eternal reflection
of drowned bodies
when I dip the knife of these arts
in the blood of another drama which shelters
in the refuge of your smoothest art
like an accepting spherical hand.

"I am a sensual god"
and when the sun falls
I whip beauty on the selfsame horse.

Absorbed in the original structure
of an old sacrilege again
you want to be something else to transpire
when your allergy to the world
wakes and stirs the intact fire
of the undefined hell that moves us
on this day of luxury on which we are
two daring wise angels
and deforming dilated shade.

In Goo

In Goo silver insects water in the air
invisible hands weave the sky grey
time breathing a little immortal now
on this day of grace at the exact hour

This is the eternal song of a fragile land
and the rain slipping immorally away.

Mythology

> *I who have seen you amid the primal things*
> *Was angry when they spoke your name*
> *IN ordinary places.*
>
> Ezra Pound

Mythological Astarte entered you
to see in her reincarnated cruelty
a once firm body
emptied running under hypnosis
in the wake
of your infamous spirit

Was I the one who brought you
from another surface,
necessary love?

The threads of day feel them fall
in their unwoven structure
the five cold fingers of the digital night
whose hounds pursue me
with their vigilant shadows.
And my image goes towards the night
without the light that limits it
growing in the familiar gloom.

In Twelve False Verses

1. Often black boots and their gesture
   (abandoned by the body that demands them)
2. in the posture of an act of violence
   (without the real expression of murder)
3. placed like a sign
   (of fury and nostalgia)
4. in the lightninged night
   (fading from death without an image)
5. diluted in the refuge
   (of another vision that grows)
6. of the procession of euphoria
   (knowing a drama's going on)
7. in the volcanic creation of a dream
   (origin of acute despair)
8. in the procreated idea
   (of a pair of black boots)
9. which wouldn't enter me
   (through the door of a world invading me)
10. without the curious itching
    (running through me now)
11. nailed without complaint to my eyes
    (as blind as your sterile womb)
12. that are going to sleep the sleep I don't feel.

Between Friends

The white ghost of a look
neither measures nor preserves
the glimpsed passing of slow hours
no one thought about the autopsy of fate
if this violent verb were
seed of aggression towards existence
illegal foreign force
immune to its tragedies
the flow would be intense and they'd know
the rage of my teeth doesn't kill me
with the sweet tamed rhythm
I would like.

1980 August 1979

The body concerned seeing the death of a member of this scene
Others' confusion in a world of mercury
dressed in search of harmony
colours and volume in pure heterodoxy
in the face of catastrophe the expression of mouths
the lines of our aesthetics undone
give me another dose the night is sad
Mechanics of death on the road
the secret enunciation of other names
draws shouts of primordial accents
in the darkest part of us
now we know the waters of memory
settle once more
I can smell the smoke of disorder
the fear rage breath of that day
in the strangeness of this morning mist

The hand and its shadow placed
in an old group portrait
exploring the idea in the gaze
glimpsed teeth lips
an abnormal gesture that betrays
the existence of an intention
traces of the force of hate
fate or its craziness
a light shade of future death
in the image of the victim the murderer's hands
or something in the photo that makes
a tremor of light surface in memory
the cold equation of an image
the gentle warning of a crime

If Already Dead Why Naval* Why Sea...

Men of Aran in the profile of the beginning
including us in a definition of death, in the epitaph
of rum and scurvy against the myth
of your salinity, self-control
of your own shadows,
your lethal function against structures
that pass clandestinely in discord,
so far from these *badlands* where I feel
a hysterical portland presence
castaway from Paradise Lost.

---

* *La Naval* was the name of a magazine the author helped to edit in Coruña between 1984 and 1986.

Premonition

Hated
intangible
and the veins turned
into tunnels of quiet danger
drown the body in a thousand dreams
when the light foam of shade
announces the visions
I foresee.

Like a profile of wind in the still air
an uncertain tremor persists
in the space my body invades
the light that discovers and perverts
the Gothic memory of the terror
I feel.

And turns finally into silence
among the ruins of insomnia in the morning
the most ferocious sentence imaginable
the defined fear of being
condemned to live alone
with my premonitions.

Edinburgh Edinburgh

The train bores landscapes like a louse
in the dark hair
of darkened Scotland
while the hands of another dawn
open the doors of that September day
crossing the North Sea towards the islands
reaching an *Edinburgh* in strange shade
leaving the train with an open mind
Where does the night sleep in *Edinburgh*?
To the left of the carbon diamond castle
with a black sun?
Four *teenage* punks
speckled a thousand metallic colours
my animal eye fixed on them
"No future Anarchy & destroy me"
because I love them since they're like you
hard Scottish stone that keeps me
from the contagious hypnosis of the *Highlands*
soaking the soul cold
Calvinist beer atheist whisky
Cruel magical hard
spectre of my aggressive dreams
I will return for your being
on your skin and foam of desire.

Biopsy

> *Une hache*
> *donnez une hache*
> *afin que je m'effraie*
> *de mon ombre sur le mur.*
>
> Georges Bataille

The urgency of a swoon in the impure make-up
of fear's cold metallic vibration

if the wrenched wings of disorder
suddenly relive the presence

of the insensitive bodies of other birds
in the air electrified by other feathers

in ardent almost sonorous vision
of the space penetrated by corpses

of the dank dark hell
of one who on dry land

lives with the most particular spectres
of insomnia monophobia nyctophobia wound sex toxin

lakes of poison repeated knives
on the route of disorder and suicide.

Of the cloud-speckled Marble moon
shadow of smoke virgin drowned in Saint Yeats
descending like an eagle in the motionless
presence of madness and derangement

hating those thick sweet gestures
of all your decorated flesh
the forceps of ignorance opening its mouth
on a brutal road wounded in the landscape

under the mirror moon fire stars bite
like a desert empire which concentrates
imaginary scenes structures
slowly blind footsteps in my dreams
sexual hell howling sick mind

the eyes consenting to betrayal
of my hard nostalgic cynicism
with the mock sadness that keeps me
wise spirit eternal anaesthetic
which sees the false door of paradise
or failure in every living being
and inside its dread an impure name.

Dyn Amo and Steve Dwoskin at Thirty

Perfection was a fragile intuition
where a defined virus lived
in every movement interpreted
by the skin's aesthetic discourse
Talc and carmine
subcutaneous seduction
the entrails' original atrocity
gestural fury in each of her nerves
in that night's striptease session
Confused the image of her lips
flying over Europe
Life a succession of light and shade
the secret of purest perfection
just a flicker of doubt in one gesture
a slight distortion in one of her movements
fleeting expression of lucid terror
in the eyes and mouth
that was definitive perfection.
The eyes and nipples fell then
with the fury of her sudden vision
everything she could pluck out happily irate
with the simple strength of her hands
and the power of one discovering the truth.

Poem to Ánxel Fole

And telluric liquids, the land
that dreams of itself and becomes
legend.
Winter murmur
summer in the flight of wasps to the sun
and fire with the oil lamp's vicious liturgy
lethal shadows
in the warm perspective of hearths
ceremony of childhood intrigues
Something to believe something
auto-da-fé.

Land and more wild land
wild but tame and cruel
violent, visceral,
secret, infamous, immemorial,
loved, fole, the land
ánxel, fole and death
death ánxel death
in you
the end.

Inlisboninsligodublin

for Piedad with love
against myself
and always

Another day against time and I degenerate
into eruption of the bed, antimatter
if already dead I feel you and do not renounce
your pain poured into the bathtub
bound between two layers of silence
reconverted to transit which bores
the weak wall separating us
perpetual love, sordid nostalgia
between the meek tremor of inhabited water
and the slow liquidity of murder
I do not renounce your always
ich liebe dich.

The Stuff Dreams Are Made of

For you to survive with the necessary force
to rise in shadow of what I was
Without you to go back to being me
orphan of another destiny
resigned to echoing your absence
life and death in intermittent parade
Humbly to be nothing for you
a fleeting figure in the shadow
of the same matter as our dreams
with the intoxicated spirit of nostalgia.

Poem for P.
Thirty-One Years on the Way to Heaven

If death is a necessary incident
which penetrates me silent without fury
treacherous and uniformly cruel
with the sweat created at nights by the failure
of a body that knows its dominions
conquered by the ongoing
offence of facts.
And so the fear I no longer feel for you
will excuse my defeat.

Elegy to a Fraternal Spirit.
Pastime in Alphabetical Order

Austria, Bernhard, Contagion
Thomas Bernhard, Disorder
Effects of illness, Bernhard
Failure, Grünkranz, Bernhard
Hochgobernitz, Inferno, *Ja*, Bernhard Yes, *Ja*
Korrektur, Thomas Bernhard
Likely Madness, mortality, Not
Österreich, Bernhard
Poem, Quite, Bernhard
Roithamer, just Roithamer, just So,
"if he should commit suicide one day", Bernhard
"and he just smiled and said Yes"
Bernhard, Trace, Thomas, Bernhard, I have
Unless Vestige, Bernhard, of Wittgenstein in you
X, Y, Z, Bernhard, The End.

Another Love Poem

He no longer felt anything lying there
nor did she when she saw him.
She wondered had she ever loved him
as she watched his blood dripping on the carpet
she, always she, would have to clean
when they took him.

I Wonder When

Force is always the same in another's body
and mortal illness what I need
to love you from afar
while I can.
I no longer see anything around me
that means more than my shadow
In dreams I defined myself as an apparition
that slits its veins in public
feeling before me
a solid invisible
full stop
in the air.

A Virus' Smooth Skin

> *A bed in the corner*
> *The suffering suffragette*
> *Such an obvious trap*
> *Imagine that*
> *A Butterball turkey*
> *Spread her body*
> *Naked and silly...*
>
> John Lydon/Keith Levene

I
(*Intonarumori*)

Falling bellows raining
in a dance of inconstant turns
with music of strange mathematics
geometric demolition
in this invasion of frightened shade
disappearing with the smoke force and rhythm
towards a window open
to the grey cold
Knowing it provokes
in the fusion of that effort in the fall
with the dominant smoke
intransigence
Always conspiracy of two matters
of classical similar purity
end of combustion
and an expression of conducted clouds
Or smoke in spirals
towards the rain waiting
for the blow and inevitable
destruction.

II
(*Prepared piano*)

To neutralize the lines
external projection
of internal forms
with a distant gaze
at what I pick from them
in the liquid of the necessary idea
Let the pigment take off
without destination
unaware of their presence
and a verminous murmur
of the fading impression
let the body invent
To show there are distances
philosophical principles
in a body exposed to everything
which do not yield and welcome
a certain false reflection in their essence
Surface that floats on the structure
skin body's organic illusion
So life shatters into minutes
as it overtakes itself
a step is indifference
and then nothing
A virus' smooth skin
when the blood is visible
the flesh becomes certain
in profiles that are lost
once I close my eyes
and leave untouched space for another try

III
(*Ondes Martenot*)

Diagonal programmes
in slow threads
and steps traced
in a square
The ardent light a lurid abandon
in the process of arming this destiny
in invisible keys
directions
I draw it *a priori*
in the infested air
A man anticipates the route
by coming from the left and believing
in the one approaching him with no intention
his gaze fixed on his goal
Two cold women
who both describe the space with their steps
towards the square's magnetic north
together crossing the intersection
of two men unused to adventure
And that's it they leave
with their shadows' introspection
The grace that is lost
in the inevitable absence
two pairs of clear eyes smiling
recalling or desiring
any distortion
of the idea planned
by a being they do not see
unaware of them
with the sun at that hour burning

concepts of quantum mechanics
the strategy agreed on the suburban
square's stage set
Four lines of steps that intersect
following the chosen directions
at the pessimistic hour
the *après-midi*
chasing a choreographic image
when the factory sirens
howl in a unanimous gesture.

Könnte ich abschalten

Könnte ich abschalten? Well
a day of that rainy november, a year
a day filled with rain in august raining
november raining was that day
the day that only Oh yes another rainy day
that that that month because ra rain rained
for me to look forward to death
perhaps
etc...

What Is Galicia?

(TV script broadcast by Galician Television on July 25th, 1988)

Galicia... date
Run...

a. wAter. Air.
   Amnesia of the conquered, Attraction of the Abyss, the tree at the foot of the tree and the hAppiness of surrounding space.
   The Atlantic is the soul, and the cliff the body of its Atrocious cAll.
b. Baroque: daily Beauty made matter in stone Beside the omnipresent wood.
c. Calm.
   Castelao, Curros, Cunqueiro, Culture, Celebration and guilt: a Celtic awareness of the Cosmos.
d. Difficult to Define that pain, to Dissuade Destiny and keep Desire useful.
   (Deluge)
e. Spiral in sphErical spacE.
   Emigration: the incEntive of our inner Exile that takes us East towards Europe, over the sEa towards succEss and illnEss, and Ever to the spirit's Eternal Estrangement.
f. Hearth. Fantasy. Factories, Fever, Future Forms, past Figures. The atmospheric phenomenon of Felicity, and all tomorrow's Festivities...
g. Granite Graphics, water and silence, where the soul of the Gulf stream Gets out. The Groan of baGpipes and characteristically Generous presence of Grease.

h. History: Herbicidal oblivion.
Humidity, *Horror vacui* and Humbleness stop us turning History into Heroism. Our inHeritance trained in flight, with the wisdom of old wounds, conquered only by ourselves.
i. Irony: the art of turning the Inferno into a wInter's tale.
j. Oriental sound. Southern rotundity.
k. Kilowatts per flooded ground.
l. Mourning: bLots on the Landscape, bLack baLLs on green feLt.
m. The Mystery of Music Makes Mortals, but the Miño takes that Mystery out to sea.
n. North. Night. Mist. Black: National poetic material.
ñ. Nh/gn/ñ.
o. West: "Galicia heeds and Obeys the call of the Occident" (Otero Pedrayo). So many centuries of Offences and Oblivion create antibodies in a people's Organism, and the Ongoing Offence of history will produce in this peaceful people's sense of hOnour the destructive Oxygen of cOntempt, an Obsession with failure and guilt.
p. Poetry. Patriotism. Passion.
Danger of extinction, lost in our own Purity, of the need to be a People. Our indifference will feed the Process of self-genocide we are exPeriencing.
Scattered landscapes, threaded between the Profiles of the Past, with the Presence of a vegetal sensation of Perpetuity. Passion and Punk Poses, Postmodern reflections and early hours on the urban Piers of night.
q. Chemistry of pain fear's Quintessence. Who's that laughing next to me?

r. River: life's Rumour, water's Religion.
Laughter always Rises where calm Reigns, in the deep Rest of one who knows the Risk and controls it.
Rural: Rural blood flows through these veins; and if Reason ever puts up Resistance, the Galician Recognizes himself in the land, in the tree's slow vitality, in the grass' invincible Resignation.
s. The Sound of Solitude and Silence. The Savage Sarcasm of present dreams and the Silent attraction for Suicide: the Sil.
The Miño is our blood, and the Sil its Shadow.
Serene and Shadowy, in the end the astute Smile transcends.
t. EarTh.
And Time, disorder and its Tenebrae. The Tradition of sad Tenderness.
The earTh is the beginning, and everything exists on and for it.
u. Utopia: to combine desire and the need for our dreams.
v. Cows in wet Valleys and the iron will of old people chained to the earth, the Vice of their sceptical fatalism. Green, green and more green on top of other greens. And behind that: Verdant.
w. Whisky: urban night.
Is Galicia Wagnerian, or a landscape-sick Wolfgang Amadeus Mozart dreaming of Sibelius?
x. eXactly July 25th.
y. Yes.
z. The End.

Last Poetry of Love and Illness
1992-1995

To my people, those of my blood
inherited or shared in parallel lives.
To all, especially the women among them, who
reaffirm me in the life and words that follow...

(Shortly before dying, Raymond Carver
wrote the following late fragment:
"And did you get what
you wanted from this life, even so?
I did.
And what did you want?
To call myself beloved, to feel myself
beloved on the earth."

I also could say the same…)

1. Posthumous Poems (1992-94)

> *And you, what side of my body*
> *were you on, soul, that you didn't help me?*
>
> José Ángel Valente

Curiosity

Knowing one is close to death
and the body is a battleground:
brain butchery.

Would you allow me, deserted love,
in this penitent fever to open
the final door, close it
behind me, sleepwalking, impassive,
or would you stick your foot
between it and destiny?

November 92

(All this to make of life a painless dose
of true existence, with its sun and shade;
and of the eternal or *big sleep*, another,
smaller one...)

If I Should Die Before I Wake

The past rots underground
and the present doesn't flow,
it's a dead river.

But this time there will be no resurrection
and the future is necessarily foreign to me.

December 92

(To believe in myself again would be the easiest thing,
but to pretend I don't believe in my return to the world
is more sensible.
I trust in my eyes, however, and know
what they can see)

Pain Leaves and Sleep Arrives

I now believe I could
walk among foreign spirits
without treading on their innermost dreams.
I no longer feel that stubborn pain
which used to inhabit my nights,
waking at one of the darkest hours

being aware the following day
would not bring anything much different
from the failure melting me
with the flames of the hell I lived in.

November 94

("Now I am become Death," said Oppenheimer
on seeing
the effects of the atomic bomb he'd helped to create,
recalling the line from the Bhagavad Gita:
"Now I am become Death, the destroyer of worlds."
This is something similar)

Acrostic

All
I wanted was to
deposit something of myself on earth that would
survive

aware I should not have let on
I was simply a
damnable interlude between two walls of
silence

all I could do living in the shade was not
inoculate for ever the one I loved with lethal
doses of the love that poisoned her
soul with eternal pain

abandoning desire for exile
I began the journey without return to the
depths of an inner
sentimental annihilation.

November 94

(War of attrition. Psychological warfare.
Passive resistance. Frontal resistance.
And rebellion, shock.
And then the impasse, Cold War.
But the aim is always victory or death.
The vigil will have to be constant and rigorous…)

From the Surface of a New Unexpected Rescue

Flooding my eyes must have been the light
of life snatched from nearby death
but everyone touched me with incredulity
taking my hands.
All those who had loved me dead
loved me more alive.
Two doors had opened in opposite directions.
I chose the one leading to life
the sun pouring in through the windows.
I would have to renew myself
return to my own life
without becoming reinfected with myself.
I would revise the script
change character again
taking up my lost
apprenticeship.

December 94

Le vent se lève!... il faut tenter de vivre!

Paul Valéry

Checking for Damage

My right hand on my body's right,
my left hand on the left.
In full possession of my faculties,
my head in the centre of the world,
I would have my slender prudent dreams
take a different line.

December 94

2. Light and Shadows of Love Revived (1995)

*to You, unique from by and for always,
whatever you do, wherever you are*

*for Her, who renewed me without pain between poems,
everything I can and still have*

*by Her, Her and Her,
next to me always, and I in them*

*and to all those ladies who were are and will be
object and cause
of this unlimited reviving love*

*(and after the last love song, I wrote
all this for them, for her, for you…)*

I

Immersion in silence is what distinguishes
those who love with a suicidal spirit
from those who are just
a brief dream.

On the nocturnal journey we undertake
through the interior of a different body
an act of love is an urgent flow
of sweat tears and sperm
against fear

unarmed words
desires that are lost
in the mist of a thousand nights
between the sheets rumpled
by the ferocious present
of two bodies which forget.

June 95

II

He gauged the distance well and jumped
overcoming the resistance
of time imprisoned
in its shadows.

He easily cleared
the wall of his beloved's dreams
and entered that foreign garden
with his hell inside
and nothing else.

June 95

(In love, as in war, we never hear the shot fired in our direction. Death, like love, never warns us which way it's coming…)

III

In love again
with the love inside me
the raging thirst for a future
has exhausted my possibilities
leading me straight towards impact:
a missile frozen in the air
feet away from a cold heart
and I'm waiting for the slightest sign of heat
to open its skin and enter the blood
overcome by the force of desire
blindly without heed
to the possible disaster.

June 95

(In the 1940s, David Lean filmed
Brief Encounter, a love story with
railway smoke and the right amount of humidity.
I am living now from these and would prefer
to keep those few intense
brief encounters than to overturn my past,
revealing a nicer present and a
possibly revived, solid
and failed future)

IV
(Brief encounter)

You flew over my airspace one day
lightly stroking me with your feathers
and disappeared with a lessening roar
like the vision of some failed
dream.

June 95

*My heart is with him who one day,
the brief gloss gone, the grace that sustained him withdrawn,
at a hostile low ebb everything that makes
reality sweet, life bearable, light adorable,
is able to declare, "Never mind!"*

Carlos Bousoño, "Partisan Heart"

V

What can I offer the one who attempts me?
Numbered days of inert passion
and eternal love always shared
with the debt owing to an existence
redeemed for usurious payments
conjugating the verbs "live" and "love"
in the first person plural
reduced to the forms of the present.

What can I offer the one who attempts me
if I'm a loose thread of the hope
Penelope weaves
and unweaves?

June 95

(Am I to be like Nerval,
"the Dark One, the Widower, the unconsoled,
the prince of Aquitaine whose Tower is abolished?"
Everything is written.
Whatever the result of my cautiously positioned
dream, I am always prepared
to embark on my slow boat to China,
loved or unloved…)

VI

Sleepless nights like damp sheets
in the circumvolutions of my brain
hung out in the wind of danger
eruption and eternal combustion
of another desired skin that would burn
in the flames its vision ignited.

Year after year I am a nest for
migratory birds
seeking warmer climates
in forced exile for the winter
conquered unarmed and captive
their wounded hearts perplexed
which pain tinges with a cold hatred.

One season in hell, another in
the temporarily pleasant, clear sky,
and at the end the sad pulchritude
of another dress rehearsal for the big sleep.

June 95

(So many years since a skin that wasn't mine,
or at least wasn't part of my eyes, explored,
known or shared,
observed me…)

VII

Seeing those two throbbing eyes
like the vision of a half-glimpsed image
in her breast in perfect symmetry
with an inner tremor that fascinates me
I should like to enter her and shelter
in her secret body for ever
protected from death
with her life

a moist shiver streaks through my body
kissing my vertebrae with fury
in a vertigo of pain and tenderness.

June 95

(I know, and you know: *"je t'aime comme on chie, je t'aime comme on chie, je t'aime comme on chie..."* as you want me to love you from now on, only true story I had)

VIII

You left your presence in my body
pouring your charm into my eyes
which won't mist over again
because nostalgia turned into a corpse
won't rot any longer

and we're going to explore the geography
of our eternal love with corrections
if you'll open sweetly again
to my absent watchful love
letting me hand it to you
and then heading

for the future freely
shared with your own life
and loved for ever.

June 95

(Many years ago, Octavio Paz wrote
a sentence that served as a banner to me,
somewhere between black and red:
"The coming revolution is a fiesta,
the beginning of the beginning that returns."
I no longer believe he has any interest in the beginning of
that return
and could distort his sentence: "The coming revolution
belongs to Chiapas, the Mayan victims of the beginning
who are in rebellion, returning to a wished-for future…"
We are all Marcos! All EZLN,
in the Lacandon jungles of what we were forbidden!…)

IX
(Love and blood in Chiapas)

I'm searching for a glance
to confirm my faith in her
and advance blindly with great determination
in another just rebellion that turns
into an urgent demand for certainties
for this rebellious Zapatist heart
forced to fight for what's obvious
with a serene fury
both ancient and wise

From the love that resists the one who would repress it
with her for company as before
or on my own armed to the teeth with nostalgia
I shall let myself be invaded by Mayan blood
so she can return to her own land
or succeed in living another thousand lives
in struggle against the world
if required
breaking its neck
and diverting
history from its course
together with the usual victims.

July 95

(Absence or presence do not alter
the distance of the spirit
that has already been admitted.
And the elements of new technologies
develop our affections…)

X

Sadly I live with your absence
survive the distance by which we are denied
while skirting the border between two worlds
unsure which one will give me
the calm I ask of myself to love you
without suffering because of your indifference
to my preventive withdrawal
from a battle I know is lost
resigned to never entering you
but not to the torture of avoiding you.

July 95

(Weaknessweakness *for my love without shadows of mourning, pour mon amour sans ombres, por mi amor sin sombras,* for —Valente— "void is the air of all being, you are not, I am not, how gyrating is the body of nothingness"…)

XI
(Weaknessweakness for the light of the fallen angel)

I do not wish to hide anything about myself
she'd never know for sure
if I didn't tell her.

I could offer her the space I occupy,
the words, strength, the determination
nourished by this confused love,
each cell in a state of grace;
the conquered, captive shadows
or the suicidal energy of my sweet surrender
to the new, unexplored territory
of her recently discovered existence.
Serene and certain, I fearlessly
enter that new, unknown world
and try to solve the mystery
of her indifference,
my besotted gaze increasingly
sleepwalking and defenceless.

She has to know everything she doesn't know
about me and my dark pretexts
before this final dream
sinks into the ocean of nothingness.
But she will remain absent or permanently protected
from the death on stand-by accompanying me.

I would prefer her to inherit what I still had
before betting life, death and soul
in a single game I lost;

and when the bailiff comes to recover the debt,
I'll give him soul and death, leaving her
the life I didn't use, which remains intact.
That way I'll stay with her:
in her body above ground,
with mine underneath it.

July 95

XII
(*Prayer*)

Now close your eyes
and imagine
what you're hearing
is an atheistic prayer
addressed to you in the darkness
by an invisible voice lost
in the temples of
ritualized love.

Hear how the silence is crossed
by that desperate carnal rumour
which approaches your existence nocturnally
infecting your desires with its own
penetrating you and settling
inaudibly and fatally
in your entrails.

July 95

Die beiden Türen der Welt
stehen offen:
geöffnet von dir
in der Zwienacht.
Wir hören sie schlagen und schlagen
und tragen das ungewisse
und tragen das Grün in dein Immer.

Paul Celan

(… and the two doors of the world are open
it was you who opened them late at night
and we hear them slam slam slam and carry the uncertain
and carry the green into your always (full stop) black
milk of the dawn we've been drinking drinking drinking
you and I for years Celan…)

XIII
(Triangulations)

The sky in two halves transfused
in your pleasant womb always open:
she and I in perfect communion
entered your life
and took up residence.

An initiatory perverse triangle
serene and without suffering
beautifully altruistic
and brutal.

July 95

(Against death! the love that goes
with me; against time running out! your
time; against mourning! desire; against
the world! a carefully planned bomb; against me!
to be the one I was, which wasn't
exactly me...)

XIV
(Against death the love that goes with me)

From the days fortune has kept for me
every one of its nights left to live
would be the last
the only essential one
if I could live you as well
crashed on your peaceful body
cohabiting your dreams
having survived my inexistence
dreamed in your nights
or prolonged in you.

July 95

(Apollinaire?... apollinaire,
apolligram, calligraire Madame Sosostris
dealt me my cards. And I made a poem
in the shape of a womb.
I must daydream in
everything that's erotic on earth.
Be nice, slightly perverse:
and make the most of Beauty's
gratuity)

XV

        Soir. La femme qui est derrière moi
        me regarde à travers du miroir que j'ai
devant ma face. Soir. Et le soleil brûle nos âmes.
Le désir chante. Et moi, maintenant, tout heureux d'être vivant.
I love you. Soir. Evening. The woman behind me watches me
in the mirror I hold before my face. Evening.
The sun is burning our souls. Desire sings.
And I now, happy still to be alive.
Je t'aime. Evening. I write
this calmly, am still
the same, at least
I think so.
Yes.

July 95

One of Mahler's *Lieder* would be the soundtrack:
"Nun will die Sonn' so hell aufgeh'n",
sung by Christa Ludwig
… for example.
(Treatment for lovers, when
"night goes dark in every bone", for example.
But I have reasons, movements, gestures,
to feel happy and satisfied; and also
to imprint the car on everything
I lost on the return journey)

XVI
(Haematic analysis of love)

With the love that comes
between you
and my fear
there's a change in the organic parameters
of my delicately balanced well supervised
and restored remains.

I could make a bitter *Lied*
dedicated to my closest beings
modifying my CD4
and lowering the level of prothrombin
in this body floating in endorphins
without syringes or drugs
to take them away.

A thirst to dream increases fever
and causes invisible haemorrhages
banishing red corpuscles from the blood.

But tears lubricate desire
provoke more nostalgia
and anaesthetize.

Friendship protects and love heals
hatred infects and wounds
indifference kills.

Once this fire is out survive free
of the final throes of one who loves you.

July 95

("I appeared before you then
and entered into your suffering
as if you were rubbish and could endure me…"
wrote Bernhard in an early poem.
Did you really forgive me so quickly?
Your death is not my death, and vice versa.
I curse the pain I carry in every cell! Because
despite my attempts to be always elegant
and to know how to keep my distance,
I couldn't help you sharing
the worst choice I ever made)

XVII
(Precaution)

She refuses to hear my old voice
and listens carefully to more recent ones
with a vague hope in the future
and fear of finding out once again
that death was hidden in them as well.

She listens closely to those other voices
and meanwhile seeks shelter in a present
that is vitally on the defensive.
She keeps the past under lock and key
maintaining her mute
discourse.

Go ahead, refuse and deny my old voice!
I now know something I didn't before:
it was never really mine.

July 95

(Unique for this, always univocal:
unique for everything *"almost" for ever*...)

XVIII

There are things for which she continues to be unique
like entering her life by fire and sword
with a request for help.

And when one is coming apart inside
fainting
only she arrives to cure that emergency.

Or turning an impulsive destiny
into an unnecessary perverse
mistake.

July 95

(Because I, like Charles Bukowski, also believe
in a simple violence. Whores of my days,
cold like me at the night's end,
women of shared blood, in the same
streets, St Pauli, Papagaio, Saint-Denis, Bar
Tabac in Pigalle, Chueca, Libertad.
Are they still there?…)

XIX
(SOS aesthetic moral racism)

The tenderness her ignorance gives off
in that eccentric ambiguous bone structure
smokes my spirit makes it sympathetic
to the insolent short-sightedness that precedes it,
with its radical obscene
bad taste
and impossible beauty
foreign to hers.

She could have been my daughter
blue-streaked like Joyce's
and I'd have hibernated my pain
in the protective kind observation
of her life which was painless and indecisive
or curious and hellish
coupled with mine.

July 95

Errei todo o discurso de meus anos.
Luís de Camões

XX

Mistakes made in life against the grain
led me to lose once more
for good and without regret
everything I'd thought was lost.

Invasive metastasis or obsession
with that possibly misunderstood love
neither cowardice nor egoism
was the reason that made me think
of summoning to myself this disaster
which demolished with me the evil caused.

And I'm trying to delay the definitive mistake
in a slow shipwreck
lived before
because this fatigued besotted ruin
is preparing to suffer more
assuming the prearranged fall
rushing into those inoffensive wished-for mistakes
avoiding the whirl that carries me
into the spirals of the void.

July 95

(Time, halt at my side! Space, bring me close to one of them!... But it's late for being modest. I should have accepted defeat and lowered my neck like bulls when it comes to the kill. Could I live in an anaesthetized world in which the future was the buttress?...)

XXI

Her cereal gymnastic beauty,
that cultured energy,
dermically firm,
and mentally ethereal

                comes towards me
                crosses with me
                the music
                of the air

and her life continues its journey,
indifferent,
unconcerned by my death,
my life.

And here I am
with her inside always
                sleepless
                and unredeemed
as my sole companion once more:
illness.

July 95

Be not sad because all men
Prefer a lying clamour before you:
Sweetheart, be at peace again -- -
Can they dishonour you?

James Joyce, *Chamber Music*

XXII

Lovelessness, brutal amputation
or atrophy of a mistreated dream,
should always be an intimate ritual
staged in clandestine halls.

Interpreting organic monologues
we'd fluently recite the internal pain
of our sad bones
when love dissolves in haemorrhages
of liquid aborted
desires.

July 95

(Unidirectional, yes, and irreversible.
Or bidirectional, but impossible.
From the past, with a miserable future, in the greedy
shared present, they're building
a well of desires and conditioned
dreams...
I am a short story. The end is written,
and everything I see is condemned
to outlive me)

XXIII

Unidirectional, unreal and tame,
going one way,
the love that assailed me without prior warning
when I no longer wished to defend myself.

Perverse, inoffensive and altruistic,
it was an innocuous placebo
administered to a body in defeat.

Disgusted by my time running out,
I open myself and pour my life
into that ferocious, silent, aimless love;
and the old love hidden and forbidden,
sealed and transferred
under guarantee
to someone who could no longer be eternal
trying in vain to avoid me
and not carry on sharing a single shadow
till the end.

July 95

("Dear Prudence" being played a thousand times. Éric
Rohmer in Coruña. Madrid. Nowhere. And
the elements of new technologies, a bit
old by now, have almost completely developed
our two solitary affections.
When there's another corpse
between two worlds, all this
will carry on existing. I'm an expert in such things)

XXIV
(Comedies and proverbs or a moral tale)

"Dear Prudence, dear Prudence..." Through the door
of the adjoining room, separated from mine by a long wall,
I could hear that song that meant so much
to me twenty years ago. *Dear Prudence*, yes, *dear
Prudence* splashing with music and words the
thick light of the sun dressed in dominical luxury.
The phone showed signs of life.
I answered the call and it was her
who often flew over my insomnia,
briefly,
and crucified my nights without realizing,
treading in silence on my dreams.
Her voice sounded lively and carefree, as if life
at that moment for her was
a relaxing bath of indulgence.
She finally said she was thinking of me and
loved me. That was true.
Somehow that was true, I suppose. It had to be.
Even so I know this didn't make her feel
exactly happy. Nor
knowing how much I'd loved her from the start.
But a certain cosmic sense of peace takes hold of me,
making my spirit rise,
rousing the energy dozing at my feet,
hearing her say those words. I tune in to
the radio station of her soul,
and would absorb all her suffering. I love you.
Yeah, I love you too.
And her voice withdraws at the speed of light
down a cable;

crosses coastal plains, mountain ridges, valleys
and the immobility of the sun
blazing down on the song of crickets in the solitude
of the inner plateau.
And when it reaches its destination evaporates
an Atlantic rumour
boiling on asphalt.
I think of her. I think of myself on this earth. Two
essences that are almost always absent.
Our coexistence is something intangible, like an
Éric Rohmer in our
lives: subtly describing how
grass grows around them.
Because I must love her as princes
fell in love in the tales of Grimm or Andersen,
when desire still served a purpose.
No more. No less.

July 95

XXV

Allow yourself to be devoured by the one who chooses you
now that you are a light that escaped
from the darkness you were captive to.

Allow yourself to be devoured
and fiercely prevent
your latent irrevocable shadow
coming back in to infect you.

July 95

Wer, wenn ich schriee, hörte mich denn aus der Engel Ordnungen?

Rainer Maria Rilke

(Who would hear me? You always heard me *beloved* internal friend *belovedana anabeloved*... Because while "all angels are terrifying", you were always a good guardian angel—you and Her, or Her and Her, strong angels that protect me ... because being is atrocious next to the look of a flower...)

XXVI
(A present on the feast of St Anne)

Beautiful as death invoked
you practise beauty internally
moving the most lethal unyielding shades

uncovering the presence
of traces of life
in the darkest ruins
with a single glance you abort the offensive
of approaching pain.

July 95

Cuando tú te vas
Cuando tú te vas
Te llevas mi sangre
Corriendo detrás...

Manu Chao

(Too long between two lives, without you our pain drawing daily closer to the door having heard the elevator door opening... And my body, my spirit, the dream, finally threw ballast overboard...)

XXVII

I explore you with my eyes
discover your insides
defiling your blood which I bring to my desire
I walk all over you
examine your organic
processes
kill you and die in you
more sweetly

or rather
why don't you inoculate me
poison of your teeth
sink into my blood
inject yourself into the veins
that watch?

hurting now hurt me
your pain in your desire
shouting in every bone
and your death
kill me revive me
so I can die
in the end

die in me
survive
lethal love
that is never
out of breath
with its thirst for love
and its five
senses.

August 95

3. Poems of Death Survived by Means of Passion and Sabotage (1995)

*To my dead, so many now, so beloved
and insistent in my memory*

*Der Tod stieg am Ende in das Leben herunter,
tötete viele während des Aufwachens,
ging an die Arbeit, müde, ungerührt.*

Thomas Bernhard

("Death finally stepped down to life,
killed many as they awoke,
set to work, tired, unmoved.")

No to transmigration into another species.
No to the afterlife, in heaven or hell.
No to being absorbed by some divinity.

[…] My bet's on unbeing. Something sure.

It rejects another existence, now I've consumed
my helping of this indigestible stew.
Not again. Once is too much already.

José María Fonollosa

Transmigration

This energy will never end,
it wasn't created nor will it be destroyed.
It will occupy different lives,
turning into foreign emotions
tattooed on other parallel bodies,
in simultaneous constant
processions.

In a warm passionate universe
I mete out doses to myself with usury,
till it's time to return,
tired and happy,
to the starting point.

August 95

*I've been born twice: the first time by my mother,
and then by myself. What a struggle, what darkness,
what writing, to be able, having once been born,
to be born again, by myself.*

*[...] I've cut the cord of my memory
from the navel of the past.*

Juan Ramón Jiménez

(Should I have cut it? Or should I have cut the flow
of my time before the inaudible, risky cry
emanating from my blood?...)

Alert and Vigilant

May life never catch me
unawares silent and neutral
and a second before surrendering
may I take with me the image of who I was when I was
 someone else
Smoke of Barakaldo Errenteria Sestao
winters in bodies from within and damp iron
in steel of Bilbao estuary the Ruhr crossed
on Deutsche Bahn trains touching flesh of
St Pauli
Kreuzberg hungry for kebab walking freely
in the shadow of the wall leather vodka pogo
alternative demolition in efficient revolt
The bitter smell of sweat from railway sleep at five
in the morning
with two nights' cold and two days craving for metal
Penamoa Carqueixo Vao in toilets of pain among
shavings
and a thousand levels of fear layers of shivers on top of
the misery
which nailed us one by one in time
fallen in a war of architects over the fatigue
of materials
The struggle continues we are far fewer and different
hell *"sont les autres"*
us as well
so many defeats in the books of the soul and hovels
constructed from fatalism and moral humility
with the victors' scorn
And visual traces of a deaf procession of
evidence marginal and wounded accompany me without
forgetting life
swipes its knife against hatred along the blade of death
the one day after day we all strive to escape from.

August 95

(And Sartre said, "When Genet decides he wants
the Worst, he knows the Worst has already been defeated…"
I also knew this from the beginning, but
it must have been a question of priorities)

Degradation

A snowball rolls downhill,
carrying shadow and nightmares,
aiming for the lowest point
of its inexistence.

A ball of life marked with
my name and destiny,
rushing towards silence,
the path long since traced out.

Given up for dead a second time,
even hell refused to admit me,
not wanting to take my weight,
my application was turned down.

Another failure that keeps me alive
till I correct and free myself.

August 95

(And if there's still more life where this one came from,
to rob of words of love and death, I'm going to
wring its neck till it feels disgust at what
it leaves behind. But by then it will have entered
a whirl of silence and humidity,
falling quiet ever more readily…)

Declaration

To love you, life, to love you almost constantly,
though you're hard and carry in between
mercy and hatred intermittently.

You're the one who always educates and accelerates
the lethal illness of those who refuse
to ignore what you're really like:
just a comfortable insulting
journey towards death,
a useless unnecessary transit.

But ignorance saves those who do not want
to risk losing you so quickly
in exchange for agreeing not to profane you.

I could use those teeth I lost
now to defend the convictions
I reaffirm in myself.

Kind and sympathetic, if it's possible,
or a steppe wolf in exile,
I shall complete the insurgent circle
with bullets of desire.

August 95

(With a thirty-two calibre bullet
in the smallest pocket of my jeans, I know
my will is everything to choose
the moment and place. And I touch it with my fingers
all the time…)

Bad Luck

And for the first time since I knew
I was still breathing and alive
I know what it is to be afraid not to be

Interrupted during the best scene
as I was dreaming a dermic dream
of passion and beauty
with a serene distance both literary and wise

Only she could be so untimely
rude uncultured and tactless
calling me after having survived
the comfortable attraction of failure
and knowing once and for all what life was
to love and be loved.

September 95

("Where danger grows, so does that which saves," thought Hölderlin… I'm beginning to understand him)

Through the Mattress

It will come silently, stealthily, nocturnally,
arriving from below through the mattress,
between the sensed feared derivations
of a viral internal rebellion:
the inheritance I keep and treasure
as if it were my own shadow.

September 95

Circumdederunt me funes mortis.

Psalm 116

Absorta est mors in victoria. Ubi est, mors, victoria tua? Ubi est, mors, stimulus tuus?

1 Corinthians 15

(Listen, *mors*, black lady, fate, you with the scythe... I felt your sting very well, but what about your victory?...
Can you hear me?!
...
Fuck off!)

Suspicion

It must be because I'm dead
and that's the reason
I see myself now from above
at a distance of ten or fifteen feet
from my own life.

I live a cold clandestine war
in the shadow of a love that no longer degenerates
into other insurrections against myself
or degraded denial of time
and refuses admittance
to the obsession or pain provoked
by the failure that infiltrated
flowing from unhealthy drains

turning my sedated soul
into a cold septic tank mild and submissive
but alert and active
contagious and lethal.

September 95

(To laugh at life, death, and everything
man has created in his weakness
and unforeseeable capacity for cruelty.
And Yeats said, *He knows death to the bone
Man has created death*)

Another's Repeated Dream

The truth is I sometimes have the impression
which gets stronger every day
that despite the evidence to the contrary
I must have died back then

and am living a repeated dream
in the nights of those who continue to love me.

October 95

*The time is out of joint: O cursed spite,
That ever I was born to set it right!*

William Shakespeare, *Hamlet*

Long-Distance Runner Out of Breath

Fleeing from a life prodigal with renunciations
of its obese oily liturgy,
mediocre in its communal failures,
icy tears, restrained indignation

he wasn't in time to exercise
his rebellion
or carry out
his definitive revenge
against an unjust, homicidal, cruel world,
because of the uselessness of his own life

solitary, sick and weary,
death overtook him and got there first.

October 95

> *Shall I at least set my lands in order?*
> *London Bridge is falling down falling down falling down*
> *[...] These fragments I have shored against my ruins*
>
> T. S. Eliot, "The Waste Land"

(Finally, sleep overdue, having not lived very well but happy, serene and satisfied, I can go back to my corpse)

Could Be Chosen as an Epitaph

Spit on me as you pass
in front of my grave
and send a moist message
of life and necessary rage.

October 95

Index of Titles/First Lines

109	I
111	II
113	III
115	IV
117	V
119	VI
121	VII
123	VIII
125	IX
127	X
129	XI
131	XII
133	XIII
135	XIV
137	XV
139	XVI
141	XVII
143	XVIII
145	XIX
147	XX
149	XXI
151	XXII
153	XXIII
155	XXIV
157	XXV
159	XXVI
161	XXVII
29	1859 to 1861
62	1980 August 1979
56	"Absorbed in the original structure"
99	Acrostic
19	After the Cold Weather
46	Afterwards
10	*Alan's Psychedelic Breakfast*
169	Alert and Vigilant
75	Another Love Poem
181	Another's Repeated Dream
39	*Atrocity Exhibition*
77	A Virus' Smooth Skin

175	Bad Luck
61	Between Friends
67	Biopsy
25	Butterflies Are Volvos
48	*Car Crash* (of Negative Death)
43	Cartography
103	Checking for Damage
15	Children
24	Cobalt and Professor Calculus
12	Conspiracy against Lois
9	Conversation with Pablo
42	Corporal (*Je T'Aime...*)
185	Could Be Chosen as an Epitaph
93	Curiosity
51	*Dandy*
173	Declaration
171	Degradation
17	Donald Barthelme
20	Dusk in Ireland
22	Dyn Amo and Steve Dwoskin
69	Dyn Amo and Steve Dwoskin at Thirty
66	*Edinburgh*
27	*Ein Menschheitsbuch*
74	Elegy to a Fraternal Spirit
47	Ether
101	From the Surface of a New Unexpected Rescue
32	*Gothic Thought*
33	Helen Brigador, Terror of Saints
64	If Already Dead Why Naval Why Sea...
95	*If I Should Die Before I Wake*
30	Impression (*Lamentatio*) 1913-Spa
57	In Goo
26	In Leonberg
60	In Twelve False Verses
71	Inlisboninsligodublin
76	I Wonder When

81	*Könnte ich abschalten*
52	Lace of Inertia
34	Leonora in Confidence
41	Level
183	Long-Distance Runner Out of Breath
28	Lysistraphes
13	Meeting with Piedad
58	Mythology
49	Narcissism
53	Nothing
68	"Of the cloud-speckled Marble moon"
97	Pain Leaves and Sleep Arrives
31	Parade on Bright Footsteps and Corpses
50	*Penetration Prayer*
73	Poem for P. Thirty-One Years on the Way to Heaven
70	Poem to Ánxel Fole
23	Possessed Lady
65	Premonition
35	Proposition
16	—R—
55	Remorse
21	Rose Intransigent with Power
54	Six
179	Suspicion
11	That
18	*The Flowers of Friendship Faded*
63	"The hand and its shadow placed"
72	*The Stuff Dreams Are Made of*
59	"The threads of day feel them fall"
177	Through the Mattress
167	Transmigration
40	Two Minutes of Dancing Dervishes
44	*Verschwende deine Jugend*
82	What Is Galicia?
45	Who?

Jonathan Dunne translates from the Bulgarian, Catalan, Galician and Spanish languages. In 2010 he edited and co-translated an *Anthology of Galician Literature 1196-1981* for the two main Galician publishers, Galaxia and Xerais, as well as editing and translating a supplement of *Contemporary Galician Poets* for *Poetry Review*, the magazine of the UK Poetry Society. His translations have been nominated for the Independent Foreign Fiction Prize and the Warwick Prize for Writing among others. He has written two books: *The DNA of the English Language* and a poetry collection, *Even Though That*.

GALICIAN

CLASSICS

1. Lois Pereiro,
Collected Poems

2. Álvaro Cunqueiro,
Folks From Here and There

3. Celso Emilio Ferreiro,
Long Night of Stone

4. Rosalía de Castro,
Galician Songs

5. Xosé María Díaz Castro,
Halos

6. Rosalía de Castro,
New Leaves

7. Carlos Casares,
His Excellency

Lightning Source UK Ltd.
Milton Keynes UK
UKHW011506051121
393446UK00001B/337